GRATITUDE JOURNAL

90 Day Gratitude Journal with Prompts

PUBLISHING BEAUTY

Gratitude for what you have right now. Gratitude for the people in your life. Gratitude for all good things that are available to you in this moment.

Being grateful isn't an idea you stick on a Post-It note for a quick shot of feel-good. There's a reason (many reasons, in fact) why you are hearing it touted so much.

Gratitude can transform you. It can pull you from the vortex of negativity that is sucking the life out of you, and give you a renewed sense of purpose and joy.

And the simplest way to practice gratitude is to turn it into a daily habit—specifically through the book you're holding right now: The 90-Day Gratitude Journal: A Mindful Practice for Lifetime of Happiness.

The 90-Day Gratitude Journal is your personal tool for injecting a dose of positivity into your day. You can use it to focus your attention on what is going right in your life instead of focusing on everything that's going wrong.

You can use it to pause for a few minutes every day and truly appreciate all that you have.

If you make the commitment to complete the entire journal, you'll have a diary of all the wonderful things that you can be thankful for. Whenever you feel frustrated or anxious, you can review this journal and recognize that life is pretty good.

Question 1 "I am Grateful for..."

This question is based on a study by Martin Seligman that confirmed that the best way to express gratitude is to not only describe what you're grateful for, but also to take the time to consider the actions that led to this good result. When you start to see a positive correlation between your actions and certain events, you'll do more to attract these good things into your life.

The purpose here is to challenge you to be ultra-specific about what you're currently grateful for. This means you'll describe how a person, event, or item has benefited your life, and in what ways you have been helped.

Question 2 "What would make today great?"

Do you know that spent, fulfilled feeling you get when you finish an amazing day? Aim for this. If it helps, close your eyes and project yourself to the end of the day, imagining and visualizing the things that would have happened if you were feeling that feeling.

These actions do not need to be earth shattering. The key is to keep them tiny enough so you actually complete them. They can be as simple as "tell my wife I love her", "get outside today," or "smile at the barista today."

When first filling out this question, you may write a bunch of action items that you thought would lead to satisfying day, but in reality, did not. That's ok! Over time you will get better at identifying the things that make your day great and thus answering this question becomes much easier.

Question 3 "What can I improve tomorrow?"

This question should be easy to answer.

You can always do something better or improve something. Write out 1 thing you want to do tomorrow 1% better.

Don't overthink your response here. Just pick one thing that will be wonderful about the next 24 hours.

Question 4 unique, specific questions.

The last question is a "wild card" prompt. Each day, you will be asked a unique question about an aspect of your life.

We cover a variety of topics with this question, including specific people in your life, favorite memories, challenges you've overcome, and common items you've taken for granted.

- People you helped
- Comfort you feel
- Things you are learned
- Your favorite memories
- A person you love
- Fears you overcome
- Relationships you treasure
- Risks you are taken
- Sunsets you are seen
- People in your life
- A local spot you like
- Simple things in your life
- Advice you received
- Your best qualities
- Your colleagues
- Abilities you have
- Gifts you received
- Clothes you own
- Things you own
- Your accomplishments
- Music you enjoy
- Children in your life
- Birthdays you are had
- Your best friends
- A place to stay
- Your elders
- Nature you explored
- Changes you are made
- Food on the table
- Books you love
- Technology
- Your body
- Your favorite vacations
- Your heritage
- Activities you love
- The country you live in
- Water to drink
- Challenges you endured
- Places you visited
- A moment that inspired you
- Hobbies you practice
- Events you attended

> When you are grateful, fear disappears and
> abundance appears. — TONY ROBBINS

I am grateful for...

_____

_____

_____

What would make today great?

_____

_____

_____

What can I improve tomorrow?

_____

_____

_____

Describe your happiest childhood memory.

_____

_____

_____

> Act with kindness, but do not expect gratitude. —
> CONFUCIUS

I am grateful for...

What would make today great?

What can I improve tomorrow?

What is a popular song that you enjoy (and why do you like it)?

Date____/____/20___

Develop an attitude of gratitude. Say thank you to
everyone you meet for everything they do for you.
BRIAN TRACY

I am grateful for...

What would make today great?

What can I improve tomorrow?

What is one of your favorite songs from your childhood?

Date ____/____/20___

An attitude of gratitude brings great things.
YOGI BHAJAN

I am grateful for...

What would make today great?

What can I improve tomorrow?

Who is the one friend you can always rely on?

> Stop now. Enjoy the moment. It's now or never.
> MAXIME LAGACÉ

I am grateful for...

What would make today great?

What can I improve tomorrow?

What is the biggest accomplishment in your personal life?

Date ____/____/20____

I am grateful for...

What would make today great?

What can I improve tomorrow?

*What is the biggest accomplishment in your professional
life?*

> The essence of all beautiful art is gratitude.
> FRIEDRICH NIETZCHE

I am grateful for...

What would make today great?

What can I improve tomorrow?

What is your favorite memory of your father (or stepfather)?

> The smallest act of kindness is worth more than the
> grandest intention. — OSCAR WILDE

I am grateful for...

What would make today great?

What can I improve tomorrow?

What is your favorite memory of your mother (or stepmother)?

> No duty is more urgent than that of returning thanks.
> JAMES ALLEN

I am grateful for...

What would make today great?

What can I improve tomorrow?

Describe your favorite pet (or former pet)?

Gratitude changes everything. — ANONYMOUS

I am grateful for...

What would make today great?

What can I improve tomorrow?

List 3 hobbies and activities that bring you joy?

> Gratitude makes sense of your past, brings peace for today,
> and creates a vision for tomorrow. — MELODY BEATTIE

I am grateful for...

What would make today great?

What can I improve tomorrow?

What is a mistake that you've made and that ultimately
led to a positive experience?

Date _____/_____/20_____

I am grateful for...

What would make today great?

What can I improve tomorrow?

Describe a family tradition that you are most grateful for

> True forgiveness is when you can say, Thank you for that
> experience. — OPRAH WINFREY

I am grateful for...

_____

_____

_____

_____

What would make today great?

_____

_____

_____

_____

What can I improve tomorrow?

_____

_____

_____

_____

*Who is a teacher or mentor that has made an impact on
your life, and how did they help you?*

_____

_____

_____

Date ___/___/20__

I am grateful for...

What would make today great?

What can I improve tomorrow?

What do you like the most about your town or city?

Date____/____/20____

Appreciation is a wonderful thing: It makes what is   excellent
in others belong to us as well. — VOLTAIRE

I am grateful for...

What would make today great?

What can I improve tomorrow?

---

*Describe your favorite location in your house and why
you like it.*

There is always something to be grateful for.
ANONYMOUS

I am grateful for...

What would make today great?

What can I improve tomorrow?

What is one thing you've learned this week that you're thankful for?

Date ____ / ____ / 20 ____

Nothing is more honorable than a grateful heart. —
LUCIUS ANNAEUS SENECA

I am grateful for...

What would make today great?

What can I improve tomorrow?

Who made you smile in the past 24 hours and why?

Date ____/____/20____

Gratitude; my cup over f lowest. — OSCAR WILDE

I am grateful for...

What would make today great?

What can I improve tomorrow?

What is a recent purchase that has added value to your life?

> Hope has a good memory, gratitude a bad one. —
> BALTASAR GRACIAN

I am grateful for...

What would make today great?

What can I improve tomorrow?

What is biggest lesson you learned in childhood?

There are always flowers for those who want to see them.
— HENRI MATISSE

I am grateful for...

What would make today great?

What can I improve tomorrow?

List 3 ways you can share your gratitude with other people in the next 24 hours

Happiness is itself a kind of gratitude. — ANONYMOUS

I am grateful for...

What would make today great?

What can I improve tomorrow?

Describe your favorite smell.

> Living in a state of gratitude is the gateway to grace. —
> ARIANNA HUFFINGTON

I am grateful for...

What would make today great?

What can I improve tomorrow?

Describe your favorite sound.

Date _____/_____/20_____

My day begins and ends with gratitude. — LOUISE HAY

I am grateful for...

_____

_____

_____

_____

What would make today great?

_____

_____

_____

_____

What can I improve tomorrow?

_____

_____

_____

_____

Describe your favorite sight

_____

_____

_____

> Walk as if you are kissing the earth with your feet. —
> THICH NHAT HANH

I am grateful for...

What would make today great?

What can I improve tomorrow?

Describe your favorite taste

Things must be felt with the heart. — HELEN KELLER

I am grateful for...

_____

_____

_____

_____

What would make today great?

_____

_____

_____

_____

What can I improve tomorrow?

_____

_____

_____

_____

Describe your favorite sensation

_____

_____

_____

Date ____/____/20____

Forget injuries, never forget kindnesses. — CONFUCIUS

I am grateful for...

What would make today great?

What can I improve tomorrow?

How can you pamper yourself in the next 24 hours?

> Thank you' is the best prayer that anyone could say. I say that one a lot. Thank you expresses extreme gratitude, humility, understanding. — ALICE WALKER

I am grateful for...

What would make today great?

What can I improve tomorrow?

Name and write about someone you've never met but who has helped your life in some way.

> Gratitude is the fairest blossom that springs from the soul.
> — HENRY WARD BEECHER

I am grateful for...

What would make today great?

What can I improve tomorrow?

How is your life more positive today than it was a year ago?

Date ___ / ___ /20___

I am grateful for...

What would make today great?

What can I improve tomorrow?

What do other people like about you?

Date ____/____/20___

So much has been given to me; I have no time to ponder
over that which has been denied. — HELEN KELLER

I am grateful for...

What would make today great?

What can I improve tomorrow?

List 3 skills you have that most people don't possess

> There is so much to be grateful for, just open your eyes.
> — ANONYMOUS

I am grateful for...

What would make today great?

What can I improve tomorrow?

Describe the last time someone helped you solve a problem at work

Date ____/____/20____

I am grateful for...

What would make today great?

What can I improve tomorrow?

What is your favorite part of your daily routine?

Date____/____/20____

Silent gratitude isn't very much use to anyone.
GERTRUDE STEIN

I am grateful for...

_____

_____

_____

_____

What would make today great?

_____

_____

_____

_____

What can I improve tomorrow?

_____

_____

_____

_____

What is a great book you've recently read?

_____

_____

_____

> The roots of all goodness lie in the soil of appreciation for
> goodness. — DALAI LAMA

I am grateful for...

What would make today great?

What can I improve tomorrow?

What is your favorite holiday, and why do you love it?

Gratitude is the sign of noble souls. — AESOP

I am grateful for...

_____

_____

_____

_____

What would make today great?

_____

_____

_____

_____

What can I improve tomorrow?

_____

_____

_____

_____

What is your favorite TV show, and why do you love it?

_____

_____

_____

> Every blessing ignored becomes a curse. —
> PAULO COELHO

I am grateful for...

What would make today great?

What can I improve tomorrow?

What is your favorite movie, and why do you love it?

Date ____/____/20___

> Through the eyes of gratitude, everything is a miracle. —
> MARY DAVIS

I am grateful for...

_____

_____

_____

_____

What would make today great?

_____

_____

_____

_____

What can I improve tomorrow?

_____

_____

_____

_____

What is your favorite way to enjoy nature?

_____

_____

> This a wonderful day. I 've never seen this one before. —
> MAYA ANGELOU

I am grateful for...

What would make today great?

What can I improve tomorrow?

Write about a recent obstacle you faced and how you overcame it.

Date _____ / _____ / 20 _____

I am grateful for...

What would make today great?

What can I improve tomorrow?

Describe a favorite pet and what you love(d) about it.

> If you are really thankful, what do you do? You share.
> — W. CLEMENT STONE

I am grateful for...

What would make today great?

What can I improve tomorrow?

List 3 things you are looking forward to in the next year.

> Three meals plus bedtime make four sure blessings a day.
> — MASON COOLEY

I am grateful for...

_____

_____

_____

_____

What would make today great?

_____

_____

_____

_____

What can I improve tomorrow?

_____

_____

_____

_____

What do you love most about your country?

_____

_____

Date ___/___/20___

> Gratitude is the most exquisite form of courtesy.
> — JACQUES MARITAIN

I am grateful for...

What would make today great?

What can I improve tomorrow?

What is your favorite food you love to indulge in?

Date ___/___/20__

> The struggle ends when gratitude begins. — NEALE
> DONALD WALSCH

I am grateful for...

What would make today great?

What can I improve tomorrow?

Write about someone who makes your life better.

> When we give cheerfully and accept gratefully, everyone is
> blessed. — MAYA ANGELOU

I am grateful for...

What would make today great?

What can I improve tomorrow?

If you're single, what is your favorite part about being single? Or if you're married, what is your favorite part about being married?

Date _____/_____/20_____

I am grateful for...

_____

_____

_____

_____

What would make today great?

_____

_____

_____

_____

What can I improve tomorrow?

_____

_____

_____

_____

*What is today's weather, and what is one positive thing
you can say about it?*

_____

_____

Gratitude opens the door to the power, the wisdom, the creativity of the universe. You open the door through gratitude. — DEEPAK CHOPRA

I am grateful for...

What would make today great?

What can I improve tomorrow?

Describe a weird family tradition that you love

May you wake with gratitude. — ANONYMOUS

I am grateful for...

What would make today great?

What can I improve tomorrow?

When was the last time you had a genuine belly laugh,
and why was it so funny?

Date ___/___/20___

I am grateful for...

What would make today great?

What can I improve tomorrow?

What body part or organ are you most grateful for today

Date ___/___/20___

> Gratitude turns what we have into enough. — AESOP

I am grateful for...

_____
_____
_____
_____

What would make today great?

_____
_____
_____
_____

What can I improve tomorrow?

_____
_____
_____
_____

What is a major lesson that you learned from your job?

_____
_____
_____

> He is a wise man who does not grieve for the things which he has not, but rejoices for those which he has. —
> EPICTETUS

I am grateful for...

What would make today great?

What can I improve tomorrow?

List 3 items that you take for granted and that might not be available to people in other parts of the world

Date ___/___/20___

Find the good and praise it. — ALEX HALEY

I am grateful for...

What would make today great?

What can I improve tomorrow?

Write about a recent time when a stranger did something nice for you.

Date _____/_____/20_____

I am grateful for...

What would make today great?

What can I improve tomorrow?

What is the hardest thing you've had to do which led to a major personal accomplishment?

> What separates privilege from entitlement is gratitude. —
> BRENÉ BROWN

I am grateful for...

What would make today great?

What can I improve tomorrow?

What is one aspect about your health that you're grateful for?

Date____/____/20___

> The more grateful I am, the more beauty I see. —
> MARY DAVIS

I am grateful for…

What would make today great?

What can I improve tomorrow?

Who can you count on whenever you need someone to talk to and why?

When it comes to life the critical thing is whether you take things for granted or take them with gratitude. — G.K. CHESTERTON

I am grateful for...

What would make today great?

What can I improve tomorrow?

Describe the last time you procrastinated on a task that wasn't as difficult as you thought it would be.

It is not joy that makes us grateful, it is gratitude that
makes us joyful. — DAVID STEINDL-RAST

I am grateful for...

What would make today great?

What can I improve tomorrow?

*What is your favorite habit, and why it is an important
part of your daily routine?*

Date_____/_____/20____

I am grateful for...

What would make today great?

What can I improve tomorrow?

Describe a "perfect day" that you recently had.

We must never forget the importance of gratitude.
— ANONYMOUS

I am grateful for...

What would make today great?

What can I improve tomorrow?

What is a favorite country that you've visited?

> Gratitude is not only the greatest of virtues but the parent
> of all others. — CICERO

I am grateful for...

_____

_____

_____

_____

What would make today great?

_____

_____

_____

_____

What can I improve tomorrow?

_____

_____

_____

_____

Describe a funny YouTube video that you recently watched.

_____

_____

Date ___ / ___ /20___

Feeling gratitude and not expressing it is like wrapping a
present and not giving it. — WILLIAM ARTHUR WARD

I am grateful for...

What would make today great?

What can I improve tomorrow?

List 3 qualities you like about yourself

Date _____/_____/20_____

What are you grateful for today? — ANONYMOUS

I am grateful for...

_____

_____

_____

_____

What would make today great?

_____

_____

_____

_____

What can I improve tomorrow?

_____

_____

_____

_____

What is one thing you look forward to enjoying each day after work?

_____

_____

_____

We must find time to stop and thank the people who make
a difference in our lives. — JOHN F. KENNEDY

I am grateful for...

What would make today great?

What can I improve tomorrow?

What was something you did for the first time recently?

> Wear gratitude like a cloak and it will feed every corner of your life. — RUMI

I am grateful for...

_____

_____

_____

_____

What would make today great?

_____

_____

_____

_____

What can I improve tomorrow?

_____

_____

_____

_____

What is what one lesson you have learned from rude people?

_____

_____

_____

May the work of your hands be a sign of gratitude and reverence to the human condition. — MAHATMA GANDHI

I am grateful for...

What would make today great?

What can I improve tomorrow?

When was the last time you had a great nap where you awoke feeling fully refreshed?

Date ___/___/20__

> The deepest craving of human nature is the need to be appreciated. — WILLIAM JAMES

I am grateful for...

_____

_____

_____

_____

What would make today great?

_____

_____

_____

_____

What can I improve tomorrow?

_____

_____

_____

_____

Shower or bath? Which do you prefer and why?

_____

_____

Date_____/_____/20____

I am grateful for...

What would make today great?

What can I improve tomorrow?

Write about a time where you felt courageous

Date ___/___/20___

It's a sign of mediocrity when you demonstrate gratitude
with moderation. — ROBERTO BENIGNI

I am grateful for...

_____

_____

_____

_____

What would make today great?

_____

_____

_____

_____

What can I improve tomorrow?

_____

_____

_____

_____

What are a few ways you can appreciate your health
whenever you're sick?

_____

_____

_____

> Gratitude is a duty which ought to be paid, but which none have a right to expect. — JEAN-JACQUES ROUSSEAU

I am grateful for...

What would make today great?

What can I improve tomorrow?

What is a favorite drink that you like to enjoy each day?

Date ___/___/20___

I am grateful for...

What would make today great?

What can I improve tomorrow?

Who has forgiven you for a mistake you've made in the past?

When I started counting my blessings, my whole life
turned around. — WILLIE NELSON

I am grateful for...

What would make today great?

What can I improve tomorrow?

*List 3 things you have now that you didn't have five
years ago.*

Date ___/___/20___

I am grateful for...

_____

_____

_____

What would make today great?

_____

_____

_____

What can I improve tomorrow?

_____

_____

_____

What aspects of your job do you enjoy the most?

_____

_____

Date _____/_____/20_____

I am grateful for...

What would make today great?

What can I improve tomorrow?

What is a positive aspect that you can learn from one of your negative qualities?

> The way to develop the best that is in a person is by appreciation
> and encouragement. — CHARLES SCHWAB

I am grateful for...

What would make today great?

What can I improve tomorrow?

What are a few aspects of modern technology that you love?

Date _____/_____/20_____

I am grateful for...

What would make today great?

What can I improve tomorrow?

What is a great recipe you've prepared that others rave about?

> Let us be grateful to the people who make us happy; they are the charming gardeners who make our souls blossom. — MARCEL PROUST

I am grateful for...

What would make today great?

What can I improve tomorrow?

Describe a recent time when you truly felt at peace.

> A sense of blessedness comes from a change of heart, not from more blessings. — MASON COOLEY

I am grateful for...

What would make today great?

What can I improve tomorrow?

What is your favorite quote or bit of wisdom that you like to frequently share with others?

> The best way to pay for a lovely moment is to enjoy it.
> — RICHARD BACH

I am grateful for...

_____

_____

_____

What would make today great?

_____

_____

_____

What can I improve tomorrow?

_____

_____

_____

What is your favorite sports team? Describe a cherished memory you have when cheering for this team.

_____

_____

Date____/____/20____

I am grateful for...

What would make today great?

What can I improve tomorrow?

*Are you a morning person or a night owl? What do you
love most about this part of the day?*

Date ____/____/20____

I am grateful for...

What would make today great?

What can I improve tomorrow?

What is the last thank you note you've received, and why?

Date ____/____/20____

I am grateful for...

What would make today great?

What can I improve tomorrow?

List 3 of your favorite possessions.

Date_____/_____/20_____

I am grateful for...

_____

_____

_____

_____

What would make today great?

_____

_____

_____

_____

What can I improve tomorrow?

_____

_____

_____

_____

_____

*What is a small win that you accomplished in the past 24
hours?*

_____

_____

_____

It is only with gratitude that life becomes rich. —
DEITRICH BONHEIFFER

I am grateful for...

What would make today great?

What can I improve tomorrow?

Describe one thing that you like about your daily commute to work

> We can complain because rose bushes have thorns, or rejoice because thorns have roses. — ALPHONSE KARR

I am grateful for...

_____

_____

_____

_____

What would make today great?

_____

_____

_____

_____

What can I improve tomorrow?

_____

_____

_____

_____

What is a personal viewpoint that positively defines you as a person?

_____

_____

_____

> Learn to be thankful for what you already have, while you pursue
> all that you want. — JIM ROHN

I am grateful for...

What would make today great?

What can I improve tomorrow?

Describe an experience that was painful but made you a stronger person.

Date ___ / ___ / 20 ___

> May the gratitude in my heart kiss all the universe.
> — HAFIZ

I am grateful for...

_____
_____
_____
_____

What would make today great?

_____
_____
_____
_____

What can I improve tomorrow?

_____
_____
_____
_____

What is your favorite season, and what do you like about it?

_____
_____
_____

Date ____/____/20___

I am grateful for...

What would make today great?

What can I improve tomorrow?

What's make you beautiful?

Showing gratitude is one of the simplest yet most powerful
things humans can do for each other. — RANDY RAUSCH

I am grateful for...

_____

_____

_____

_____

What would make today great?

_____

_____

_____

_____

What can I improve tomorrow?

_____

_____

_____

_____

What are you most looking forward to this week?

_____

_____

_____

Date ___/___/20___

I am grateful for...

What would make today great?

What can I improve tomorrow?

*What is an app or piece of technology that you use every
day that adds value to your life?*

It's not happiness that brings us gratitude. It's gratitude that brings us happiness. — ANONYMOUS

I am grateful for...

What would make today great?

What can I improve tomorrow?

What makes you happy to be alive?

Date ____/____/20____

I am grateful for...

What would make today great?

What can I improve tomorrow?

List 3 things you like about your job or workplace.

Printed in Great Britain
by Amazon

28734209R00056